WEIGHT TRAINING

FOR

CYCLISTS

WEIGHT TRAINING

FOR

CYCLISTS

Contributors

Fred Matheny
Stephen Grabe

also Andrew Buck and Geoff Drake

Photos by Michael Chritton
Illustrations by Jude Roberts-Rondeau

Vitesse Press
Brattleboro, Vermont

Chapters 1-5 copyright © 1986 by Fred Matheny. Chapters 6-11 copyright © 1986 by Stephen Grabe. Chapters 12-13 copyright © 1986 by Vitesse Press. Photos copyright © 1986 by Michael Chritton. Illustrations copyright © 1985 by Jude Roberts-Rondeau.

Portions of this book have been published elsewhere. A shorter version of chapters 1-5 appears in Fred Matheny's book, *Solo Cycling*. Parts of chapters 6-13 have been published as articles in *Velo-news, A journal of bicycle racing*. The illustrations are taken from *Bicycle Road Racing*.

LIBRARY OF CONGRESS CARD NUMBER 87-115125

ISBN 0-941950-11-5

Published by Vitesse Press
A division of FPL Corporation
Box 1886, Brattleboro, VT 05301

Printed at Montpelier, Vermont by
Capital City Press, Inc.

Contents

About the authors

Fred Matheny has been lifting weights since his high school and college days as a football player. An avid sportsman, he later took up skiing, mountaineering, running and cycling. He has competed in state and national cycling championships and rides as much as 9,000 miles a year. Matheny is a high school and college English teacher in Colorado and has written two books: *Beginning Bicycle Racing* and *Solo Cycling*. His articles have been published in *Bicycling, Cyclist, Velo-news* and other cycling magazines.

After a 10-year career as a biologist, Stephen Grabe recently enrolled as a graduate student in exercise physiology at Purdue University. There he also teaches weight training, exercise and fitness, and bicycling. A Master-level weightlifter himself from 1969 to 1981, he has officiated at U.S. Weightlifting Federation competitions and coached weightlifting clubs. He is a member of the American Weightlifting Coaches Association, the American College of Sportsmedicine, and the National Strength & Conditioning Association. Grabe is a licensed racing cyclist and has conducted seminars on strength training for cycling teams.

A college professor, Andrew Buck is a 1986 national cycling champion in his age group (35-plus). Geoff Drake, former editor of *Velo-news*, is a racing cyclist and triathlete.

Foreword

What is the best way for you, a cyclist, to learn about weight training? If you're lucky, your cycling coach is experienced in weight work. Or perhaps your local health center has a weight instructor who also races bicycles. Wishful thinking? Probably. It's more likely that your cycling coach only recently learned of the benefits of a weight training program, or that the closest the local weight coach has been to a bike race is watching the Tour de France on TV. Maybe you don't have any coach at all and are trying to make sense out of an exercise book written for the fitness market or for athletes in other sports.

What's a rider to do? This volume can help. In it you'll find advice on designing a weight program that suits your needs as a cyclist. Use it in combination with a detailed exercise manual or, better yet, take it to the weight center. There you'll find something recommended by the authors — an experienced weight instructor to show you how to do the exercises. Better than any drawings or photos, a weight coach can teach you how to lift safely and correctly.

After that it's up to you. Several theories and methods are presented here. Try them, and see what works for you. As Fred Matheny says, "The plan you use is less important than the fact that you are lifting." Weight training is used by top athletes in almost every sport. Now you can join them.

1.
The case
for weight training

One of the most important things you can do to improve your cycling is to train with weights. Strength development is obviously important in sports like the shot put and football, where technique will take you only so far. In fact, most discus throwers spend as much time in the weight room as they do in the throwing circle. However, endurance athletes have been slow to see how increased strength can help them to ride or run farther and faster.

Swimmers, whose training usually includes extensive weight work, have been an exception, and world records in swimming have fallen rapidly in the past few years. Now cyclists are getting in on the action. Weights are used extensively by riders at the Olympic Training Center in Colorado Springs. Former national cycling team member and world championship medalist Cindy Olavarri says, "Weight training three times a week with Olympic [free] weights is the key to my fall/winter training. I do lots of leg work: full squats, cleans, etc.—power lifting."

How does weight training help a cyclist? A strong muscle uses a smaller percentage of its total strength to do a submaximal job. Fewer muscle fibers are recruited so the muscle doesn't tire as fast. If one cyclist can squat 20 reps with 300 pounds and another can manage that many reps with only 200, the first rider uses a much smaller percentage of his total strength when he pedals. He doesn't tire as fast. Of course you also need to train on the bike so you can efficiently convert that strength in the squat into several hours of pedaling. Low-repetition, weight trained strength alone won't suffice. But neither will a steady diet of riding. You need both to approach your potential.

As a bonus, when maximum efforts are called for, as in the last leg-searing mile of a time trial or on a hill, you will have more strength to work with. Even cyclists on traditional training programs without weights have tried to build power with big-gear efforts on hills or into the wind, but weight training is a more efficient means to that end.

Why haven't more riders taken to pumping iron? Let's look at some of the dire but groundless predictions about weight training and its effect on cyclists.

The fear of gaining weight

Some riders fear that weight training will make them bulk up and leave them unable to climb. This is rarely true. The potential for developing muscle size is genetically determined. Some athletes are "easy gainers." When they start to lift, their muscles literally bloom. Their biceps split their shirt sleeves and their quadriceps threaten the seams of their pants.

Other athletes, on identical programs and investing equal emotional energy, don't get bigger at all, often to their intense dismay. They get stronger, faster, quicker — but they still look like skinned rabbits in the weight room mirror. These different reactions to weight training appear to be due to the differing levels of hormones in the body rather than to the number of sets and repetitions in the workout.

If you are genetically programmed to be stocky and muscular, a weight training program can enhance that tendency. If you have always been a lean, small-boned person, no amount of weight training will make you look like Olympic speedskater-turned-cyclist Eric Heiden.

Regardless of your body type, the strength gains from weight training more than outweigh any minor increases in size. It is your power-to-weight ratio that is the crucial factor. For example, if you weigh 150 pounds and can squat with only your body weight, your power-to-weight ratio is 1-1. If after six months of training you weigh 160 pounds and can squat with 320, that ratio has doubled.

Eastern Europeans have long known the benefits of weight training in developing the total body strength needed in cycling. This Soviet rider in a time trial stage of the 1985 Coors Classic uses his lower-back muscles to help power a big gear and demonstrates the importance of upper-body strength in sprinting out of the saddle.

The small gain in body weight has been more than offset by increased strength.

Several qualifications are in order. First, there is no reason to become a fanatic and try to look like a heavyweight powerlifter. Excessive bulk in the arms, shoulders, and chest isn't useful for a cyclist. Strength, yes, but not the kind of strength and accompanying bulk that enables you to bench press 400 pounds.

Also, though a gain in body weight may be caused by simple gluttony, the blame often falls on the weights rather than the calories. Most riders start to lift during the winter when they cut their miles down. They eat for 300 miles a week but ride only 100. The weight training gets the blame for the rapidly increasing roll around the middle.

Increasing the size and weight of your muscles is a slow process. You can easily monitor yourself to see if you are starting to get too heavy, especially in the upper body. Unlike the accumulation of fat, the development of big muscles won't occur so fast that you'll be unable to stop the process in time.

Even if you do gain muscle bulk during the off-season lifting program, you'll probably lose it automatically as you begin logging more miles in the spring. Surprisingly, when you begin to lift on an in-season maintenance schedule, most of the strength you've developed will be retained but the muscular size will decrease. It is important to tolerate some temporary muscular hypertrophy during the winter months to have the increased strength come spring. Even if you don't get all the way back to your former skinny self, you'll look better in a skinsuit.

And ultimately, it doesn't matter. Good cyclists accept their heredity, and whether thin or stocky they don't use it as an excuse. Instead they concentrate on their training programs. As Canadian professional Steve Bauer, also a world championship medalist, said after a win in 1982, "I'm not as light as I'd like to be but I'm always this way — it's just my physique."

More than leg strength needed

Another misconception, even among riders who lift, is that only leg strength is important in cycling. However, on the bike you need upper-body strength to stabilize your pedaling motion. Lower-back strength is crucial to powering a big gear. Next time you ride, touch the muscles along your lower spine as you pedal. Feel the rhythmic contractions. When you sprint out of the saddle, notice how you pull on the bars as if you are doing a power clean. Riders have ignored the most important fact in the sport: Although cycling demands total body strength, it doesn't stimulate its development. Supplemental strength training is vital.

So don't neglect your upper body if you are looking for maximum speed. A little weight training would help some riders' overall proportions, too. Some cyclists look like a Tyrannosaurus, with huge legs topped off by atrophied arms clutching the bars. All-round strength is important — remember that dinosaurs became extinct.

Europeans divided

Another objection to weight training is that the European pros don't seem to do it. If the best riders in the world don't need to lift, the argument goes, why should I? The answer is obvious — you probably don't have the potential to be a top European pro. If you merely followed Fausto Coppi's famous three-part program for cyclists (1. ride the bike 2. ride the bike 3. ride the bike), you'd get better. But not much and not very fast. Riders with more potential would start at a much higher level and improve more rapidly. Look at the selection process in Western Europe. Only the best riders survive the trip through amateur racing to pro ranks. These riders are already strong, fast, and aggressive. They may not need weight training to be competitive, but the experiences of top Eastern European amateurs suggest that it could make them more so.

In fact, one striking effect of weight training in any sport is the way it can develop an average athlete into a much better one. Well-trained athletes with natural world-class strength will always dominate. But the general level of competition in all sports has risen dramatically simply because many more athletes are strong and powerful, not just the genetically gifted ones. Think what this means for you, especially when few cyclists have begun to lift seriously. A winter of strength work could put you ahead of your competitors.

While some European professionals avoid weights, cyclists in other countries see them as vital. Many of the top Soviet road riders of the past decade are strikingly developed without reduced

Shoulder and neck muscles strengthened by weight work can help minimize the effects of a crash.

climbing efficiency. Reportedly, former world sprint and kilometer champion Sergei Kopylov owes his success to weight training. The Poles use circuit training. East German cyclists lift weights, but neither their pedaling abilities nor their competitive records in the past few years seem to have been hurt. American cyclists are in danger of being left behind both in training techniques and on the road.

Weight training and injuries

Another misinformed rap against weight training is that it causes injuries. For instance, you may have heard that squats can hurt your knees. Of course they can if they are done incorrectly, but the same can be said for cycling if your cleats are badly adjusted or the saddle is set wrong.

Weight training can also protect you from injury if you crash. A strong shoulder girdle prevents many collarbone injuries, and general upper-body development absorbs some of the shock of hitting the road. If you are strong, you can handle the punishment of the inevitable falls better and get back into your training faster.

Football players develop large powerful necks to protect them from injury, but cyclists, who are in potentially greater danger, have done nothing to strengthen this vital area. A hardshell cycling helmet can protect your skull, but only strength trained muscles can save your neck.

Other misconceptions

You may also have heard that weight training will ruin the smoothness of your pedal stroke. There is an interesting parallel here with basketball players. Five years ago, most basketball coaches were hesitant to allow their players to lift for fear it would hurt their shooting touch. Now strength-development training is an integral part of every top basketball program. The added power has increased jumping ability dramatically, and shooting percentages have not fallen.

Another reason that strength training hasn't caught on with many cyclists is because most successful riders have been thin, wiry people. They have never tried strength sports because they had little natural affinity for them. They never thought of themselves as strong athletes. We tend to gravitate toward those activities in which we are quickly successful, and few riders have body types or interests that lead to equal success in cycling and powerlifting.

It is time for riders to recognize just how much they could improve if they became stronger. I see no reason why a relatively small-boned cyclist couldn't eventually do squats in the off-season with almost as much weight as a good regional powerlifter, at least in high-repetition training. This would produce a rider of awesome strength compared to present standards and would boost levels of cycling performance proportionally if the experience in other sports holds true.

There is good news in the weight room for older riders too. Evidence is growing that progressive resistance exercise can slow down or even reverse the lowered muscle volume and strength that seems inexorably to accompany aging.

As a great example, consider body-builder-turned-bike-racer Phil Guarnaccia of California. He has done extensive weight training for years, and now on the bike he regularly defeats men 20 or 30 years his junior. At the age of 68 he won the national road championship for men 55 and over, giving away 13 years but dishing out lots of punishment. If you are an older rider, squats can build the legs that time forgot.

Of course if you want to race, you have to achieve basic cycling fitness first and this can be done only with long, steady rides. However, the realization is growing that once this base is established, maximum improvement is possible only if we establish strength and power as a top training priority.

2.
Basic exercises

Weight training offers many advantages to the cyclist. But there seems to be no agreement on the best way to develop strength, although several theories are being argued and examined. The first advocates one set of 8-12 repetitions. Proponents of this view argue that if the muscle is stressed to exhaustion in one set, more exercise will not increase the strength gains possible that day. Multiple sets, according to this theory, are a waste of time. Dan Riley, strength coach of the Washington Redskins, argues in *Scholastic Coach* (January 1982) that "one properly performed set will produce maximum gains in strength."

The second theory is the circuit training routine familiar to most American cyclists because it is advocated by former U.S. national coaching director Eddie Borysewicz. He describes it in his book, *Bicycle Road Racing*, and it is used at the Olympic Training Camp. Circuit training combines high reps, light weights, and multiple sets to improve cardiovascular efficiency as well as strength.

The third theory is an outgrowth of workouts used in competitive powerlifting. Athletes use about five sets of 3-8 reps with maximum weight in several basic exercises: squats, deadlifts, power cleans, and bench presses. The workout is done only twice a week to allow the muscles to recover and grow stronger. Notice that these exercises work the legs, hips, lower back, and chest — the power train of the body.

Finally some experts advocate machines like those made by Universal or Nautilus to isolate muscle groups effectively.

I'll explain how you might set up a training program using some of these methods. However, the plan you use is less important than the fact that you are lifting. Any well-designed program will

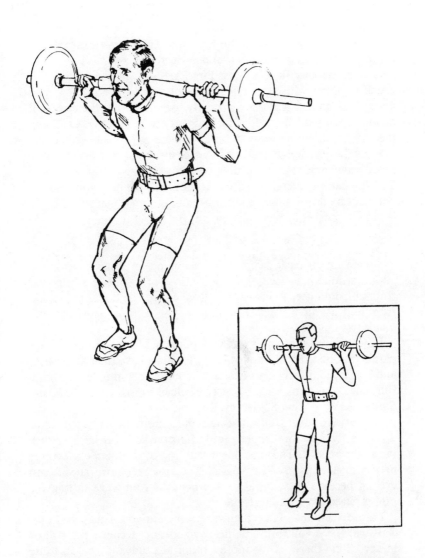

Squats develop the whole power column and are the most important weight exercise for cycling. Squat until your thighs are parallel to the floor or slightly lower, using the detailed instructions on page 39. 1984 U.S. Olympic coach Eddie Borysewicz recommends combining squats with toe raises (inset) which work the calf muscles.

produce gains regardless of the hype that emanates from some of the more commercial programs and devices.

A word on specific exercises. First, get an experienced lifter or coach to show you correct form. I'm going to assume that you know the names and can properly perform the exercises I'll mention, but personal help is the only way to be sure you are doing them for maximum benefit. A series of pictures just isn't effective.

Second, free weights are less expensive than machines, more readily available, and according to many experts, more effective. So I'll mention several specific exercises that will help your cycling but can't be done on machines. If you have to use machines, try to find the closest equivalent movement.

Squats

Squats are the basic exercise for cycling power. They develop the all-important quadriceps but they also work your whole power column from knees to lower back. Make sure you do them in good form and use light weights at first or you'll have incredibly sore quads two days later.

I recommend that you squat to a position where your thighs are parallel to the floor but no lower. Full squats have their advocates, and it is undoubtedly an advantage to exercise a muscle through a full range of motion. According to Michael Yessis, editor of *Soviet Sports Review,* the Soviet cyclists include full squats in their programs. However, full squats are much more difficult to learn to do correctly, and for inexperienced lifters the added risk isn't worth the slight benefit. The time spent learning to do them correctly is better spent riding. Also, parallel squats are more specific to cycling because they duplicate the bend in your knee during the power phase of the pedal stroke.

I also recommend fairly high repetitions for your squat workout. This will force you to use lighter weights and decrease the risk of injury, but there is a more important advantage. Exercise physiologists define power as work over time. Traditional strength tests and competition measure gains with a one-repetition maximum lift. Such strength is of little benefit to a cyclist who has to pedal thousands of revolutions in a race. But power — the ability to perform many repetitions in a short time — is obviously vital to cycling success. This being so, 50 reps in the squat are more beneficial than 10 because training is specific to athletic performance.

It may be argued that if this is true, why not dispense with squats and just ride hard in big gears? The answer is that you are building strength and power along a continuum. You have high resistance, low reps on one end (squats) and low resistance, high reps on the other (easy spinning). You need the whole range of effort in your training.

In the off-season period most riders do two squat workouts a week with three to six sets, 10-50 reps each, and moderate weights. One day, for instance, (and the weights listed are just examples) a fit rider might do a 50-rep warm-up set with 135 pounds, a transitional set of 30 reps with 185, and as many reps as possible with 215, going to exhaustion. If you choose the weight correctly, you will get 30-40 reps on the last set before you succumb.

This is intense work. To reduce the chances of burning out mentally, on the other day of the week devoted to squats do two sets of 20 with increasing weight, say 135 and 205, for a warm-up and then four or five sets of 15-20 reps with a weight 10-20% higher than the heaviest you used on high-repetition days. Try to allow as little time as possible between sets, but even that small break is a welcome mental relief. If you try to do 30-50 reps per set to exhaustion twice a week, you'll lose your enthusiasm for squats in a hurry.

Other exercises

The second important muscle group that you need to work is the lower back. Squats do some of it. Back extensions are excellent if you have the right equipment. Another possibility is the Good Morning. I like stiff-legged deadlifts with moderate weight and high reps. Whatever you choose, start very gradually and never go to maximum, since your lower back is susceptible to injury.

Next, do rowing motions to strengthen your arms and upper back. Do a bent row and notice how your position is very similar to your most aerodynamic position on the bike. Upright rows are good too and strengthen the trapezius muscles that help support your neck.

Finally do abdominal- and neck-strengthening exercises every time you lift in the early season and three times per week the rest of the year. Cycling does nothing for your stomach muscles, but if they get weak you may become susceptible to back trouble. I like crunchers, which I do while lying on my back with my legs directly overhead. I hold a 25- to 45-pound plate behind my head and curl my shoulders and upper body up as far as possible. Work up to 75 reps without weight and then add plates five pounds at a time. You can also lie on your back with your knees bent and your feet flat on the floor. Again, just curl your head and shoulders. Don't do complete sit-ups because they work the wrong muscles and lead to back problems.

Strengthen your neck with wrestler's bridges, a neck harness, neck isometrics, or on a special machine designed to work the neck muscles in all four directions.

Other useful exercises include incline presses, shoulder shrugs, hang cleans, calf raises, leg curls, leg extensions, and lat pulldowns.

Although I think squats are most effectively done using the sets and reps I just mentioned, there are many ways to organize the other weight training movements into a useful program.

3.
Circuit training

One way to incorporate your chosen exercises into a routine is circuit training. Some experienced weight training coaches dislike it, believing it to be inefficient to try to build both strength and cardiovascular function with weights. They maintain that strength is best built with a slower-paced weight training program, while cardiovascular function is improved with specific activities like cycling. In this theoretical view, modifying a standard weight program into a circuit in hopes that it will build both abilities is a waste of time.

However, circuit training is used extensively by cyclists at the Olympic Training Center under the supervision of national team coaches and in Eastern bloc countries, and it works well. In practice it seems to be a good method of increasing strength and maintaining some aerobic fitness during the preparation period (October through December).

Circuit training workouts are convenient regardless of your facilities. They can be done with free weights or on a Universal or similar machine, with calisthenics and body-weight exercises like pull-ups, or with a quick trip through 10 or 12 stations at the local Nautilus center. The only requirement is that 20-second bouts of intense work be separated by equal amounts of rest time.

It helps to do your circuit with a training partner. That way he or she can rest while you do a set, and you can encourage each other. Also the natural competition inherent in such a situation will make both of you work a little harder.

It is important to vary your circuit. Don't do the same sequence of exercises every time or you'll quickly become mentally stale and dread the workouts. One big advantage of circuit training is the variety possible. If you use your imagination, you can do circuits twice a week for months and never duplicate a workout.

It is a common fault to use too much weight. You should do about 10-15 reps in the 20 seconds and be able to get through the whole sequence without losing form or cheating on the exercise. The object is to build strength, not show it off with heavy weights to everyone else in the weight room. Don't be an exhibitionist. Remember too that your cardiovascular system is getting a workout because of the fast movement from one exercise to the next. The amount of weight you can handle will be limited by your huffing and puffing.

Do most of the movements at a steady rate. With a relatively light weight it is tempting to do bench presses, for instance, as fast as possible, squeezing in 20-25 reps in the time span. However, weight training movements should be done in a controlled manner to help you avoid injury. Pumping those weights too fast can pull muscles or strain ligaments. Equally important, if you go too fast and throw the weight up, most of the work is done by momentum. Your muscles won't be exercised through the full range of motion. So do each exercise slowly and concentrate on the muscles you are working.

Sometimes you should make an exception to this rule for the squat. To build what the Soviets call "speed-strength" you can lower to a parallel position steadily, then power up as fast as possible. Done this way they are excellent to finish off a workout of slower, heavier squats.

A simple circuit workout

Here is a simple circuit that you can do with only a 110-pound barbell set, a chinning bar, a simple bench, and about 40 square feet of floor area. (Weights given are only samples to illustrate how to change the barbell plates quickly. A drawback of doing the circuit with free weights instead of a Universal machine is that it takes longer to alter the weight. However, a little planning will enable you to change the weight in the 20-second rest period.)

1. Cleans (75 pounds).
2. Crunchers.
3. Bent-over rowing. (Use the same weight that you used in the clean.)

In sprinting, the muscles of the upper torso are used to pull on the bars.

4. Push-ups. (You can substitute dips if you have a rack.) During the rest period after this exercise, add weight to the bar in preparation for:

5. Squats (110 pounds).

6. Pull-ups. (Vary the grip each time through the circuit: palms away, palms toward you, wide grip, narrow grip, behind the neck.) After the pull-ups, take a 5- and a 2.5-pound plate off each end of the bar.

7. Bench press (95 pounds). Then take 20 pounds off each end.

8. Upright rows (55 pounds).

9. Neck bridges (for the all-important neck muscles). When they get too easy, put a weight on your chest. Pad the floor or wear an old cycling helmet to protect your head. Some people prefer a neck harness, available for $10 from a sporting goods dealer.

10. Jumping squats (75 pounds). Pad the bar with a towel for this one.

Go through the complete circuit once the first time you try it. Eventually you'll want to work up to three times through with a two- to four-minute rest between trips.

To make this circuit much more difficult, alternate a 100-yard fast run with each exercise. Or if you have a wind-load simulator, get on and ride hard for 30 seconds. Rope skipping, squat thrusts, even running in place are all possibilities. The idea is to get your heart rate up higher.

Nautilus centers, with their emphasis on fast movement from one exercise station to the next, would seem to be a logical way to do circuit training. And they are, at least in theory. But many athletes have found that the equipment is crowded and they spend too much time between exercises waiting for the next machine.

Calisthenics

If you don't have access to weights or you are traveling, you can do a respectable circuit with calisthenics. The "countdown circuit" is the best format to use. Choose about eight exercises (see listing below) and do each exercise in turn, using a predetermined number of repetitions. Repeat the circuit 10 times, decreasing the reps by one each time for certain exercises. For instance, begin with 15 push-ups on the first set, 14 on the second, and so on down to six. Here's a sample:

Exercise	Number of reps	Total number of reps for 10 sets
1. Windmills	20 decreasing to 11	155
2. Push-ups	15 decreasing to 6	105
3. Mountain climbers	25 every set	250
4. Crunchers	20 every set	200
5. Jumping jacks	25 every set	250
6. Pull-ups	10 decreasing to 1	55
7. Step-ups to bench	25 each set	250
8. Arm circles with weight (use light dumbbells, books, etc.)	20 decreasing to 11	155

As you can see, the workout doesn't look very impressive at the beginning but by the time you've sweated through 10 sets, you'll have racked up some pretty impressive numbers.

Aerobic exercise classes at athletic clubs can be excellent circuit workouts too because they are little more than calisthenics to music. Pro rider Davis Phinney says he does aerobics for stretching and flexibility. His teammate Ron Kiefel lists exercise classes as part of his off-season training.

Many fit cyclists complain that aerobics classes are good only for stretching, that they aren't hard enough to get the heart rate up. This is true if you choose a class designed for the average athletic club member. A good instructor can make a class so demanding that no one can finish. So shop around and let the club manager know what you are after.

Many clubs grade their aerobics sessions according to difficulty. Look for the toughest one. You can make any workout of this type more difficult by doing every movement as vigorously as you can and by wearing leg and ankle weights. National championship medalist Ross Potoff is another rider who uses aerobics in the off-season, in addition to Nautilus workouts. He thinks the key is selecting an outstanding instructor who is extremely enthusiastic. Another key is your attitude. As Potoff observes, "I take aerobics like I do racing — very seriously."

4.
One-set and other workouts

Another popular method of weight training for athletes is the "one set to exhaustion" technique. After a warm-up, one set of each exercise is done with a weight that allows only 8-12 reps before momentary muscular failure. Proponents argue that athletes don't have the time to train with weights several hours a day as body builders or competitive lifters do. They also argue that if a muscle is worked to exhaustion once, repeated exercises serve no useful purpose since the muscle can't be stimulated to further improvement until it recovers and is exhausted again two days later. According to this theory, multiple sets are a waste of time and energy. If you go all-out on one set, you've produced all the improvement you can for that workout. The theory behind Nautilus is similar.

This approach is controversial but has advantages for the rider with limited training time who has to be out putting in some miles and can't be spending hours in the weight room.

If you use this technique, be sure to do each repetition slowly and strictly. Concentrate on the muscles you are working. Don't cheat by arching your back in the bench press or assisting in the upright row with your legs. Ideally you should have a training partner who can spot for you. When you can't do another rep by yourself, say after nine, he or she can help you force out another three reps so you work the muscle to the maximum.

A drawback of the one-set method is the danger of mental fatigue. It's tough to push to exhaustion and you can get thoroughly sick of the whole procedure. Another problem is the idea of exercising to failure. Who wants to fail? Yet when you train this way, you fail on every exercise every day you lift. This seems to violate the "train for success" maxim. However, you have to accept the paradox inherent in weight training. Only by failing to make that last repetition do you force the muscle to grow stronger. When you lift, failure is success.

Here is a sample one-set workout for the preparation period using free weights:

1. Bench press
2. Bent-over rowing or corner rows
3. Weighted dips
4. Weighted pull-ups
5. Crunchers with weights
6. Back extensions
7. Leg extensions
8. Leg curls
9. Squats
10. Neck bridges

Remember — because of the risk of injury, don't do lower-back or neck exercises to failure.

I do this routine fairly frequently, but I do two sets of most exercises. The first is a warm-up set using lighter weights and-submaximal reps. Then I add weight and go to exhaustion on the second set. Many authorities tell you that a warm-up set is a waste of time because the warm-up that takes place during the first five or six reps of a set is sufficient. This hasn't been my experience. And quite a few people seem to get injured when they do one set to maximum without a formal warm-up of the specific muscles involved.

Of course you don't have to do any of the exercises to failure in order to get some benefit from them. But the more thoroughly you exhaust the muscle, the more improvement you'll create, as long as you allow sufficient rest between exercise bouts.

This method of weight training is especially useful during the season if you restrict it to the upper body. It is quick, so you can do it in 15 minutes before or after a ride. One set is not so exhausting that you have no energy left over to train. Yet you can increase muscle strength, even at the height of the racing season, instead of just maintaining it.

Vary your workouts to prevent staleness. Pro rider Ron Kiefel, for example, takes exercise classes in the winter. Done with leg and ankle weights, aerobics sessions can provide a demanding workout similar to circuit training.

Special workouts

In addition to the basic day-to-day programs I have mentioned, there are several specialized techniques that can help build cycling power. They are tough and demand a great deal of emotional energy, so you should use them infrequently. But if your progress has stalled, they can jolt your system so hard that you will begin to improve again if you couple the high-stress work with increased rest.

1. Try a quadricep super set. Choose a weight on the leg extension machine that will allow you to do 20-25 reps to exhaustion. First warm up, then do these strictly and slowly so your quads are burning unbearably and you can't get full extension on another rep. Then immediately go to the squat rack and do 30-50 reps to exhaustion. The idea is to exhaust the quads with the leg extensions so they are already tired when you squat. The problem with squats as a leg developer is that your back usually tires before the quads so you have to stop before your primary cycling muscles get a good workout. By pre-exhausting the quads with leg extensions, you bring their strength into line with that of your back so you can squat until the quads just can't go anymore.

2. Set an ergometer on a resistance that will allow you to maintain 90-100rpm. If you don't have an ergometer, use a wind-load simulator with appropriate gearing. Do 30 seconds all-out, alternating with a set each of squats, leg extensions, and leg curls. Repeat three times. This one works your legs in several different ways and stresses your cardiovascular system in the process. Putting the pedaling motion in the sequence of other leg exercises makes all the movements more specific to cycling.

3. Plyometric workout. Jump from a two- to three-foot-high box or platform to the ground, land on both feet, and immediately bound upward to another platform. Pivot around and repeat. Work this one gradually or your leg muscles will become quite sore. Alternate a set of 10 with a set of squats, etc.

4. Mountain or stair running. If you have been doing enough running in your off-season program to accustom your legs to the stress, some uphill running can develop great quadricep power and make you pant like an erupting volcano in the process. Pro rider Davis Phinney is an advocate of this sort of workout and does mountain running and hiking on the steep trails west of his home in

Boulder, CO. Steep mountain trails are best but any hill — pavement, grass, gravel, or dirt — will do. If you live in the flatlands, look for stairs in a big football stadium or basketball arena. Failing that, try the staircase in your local skyscraper. When it gets too easy, add a weightbelt or half a car inner tube filled with sand and draped over your shoulders.

5.
Putting it all together

Some coaches tell their riders to lift three days a week during December, January, and February, and then taper to two days in March. When racing begins in earnest they stop lifting altogether, resuming in late November. The East German riders subscribe to this method, according to their national team coach. However, most experienced strength coaches agree that it is better to do a minimum program even at the height of the season to maintain the strength you've labored so hard to build. Many studies have shown that building strength is difficult and requires two to three hard workouts a week, but maintaining that strength can be done with a minimum program once per week.

Opinion is divided on whether you should do leg exercises during the season. Most riders don't, feeling that the quads get plenty of work on the bike and the addition of the usual squats or leg extensions will overstress them and reduce cycling performance. Others do one set at midweek. Very few national-caliber riders do both because of their frequent travel and the unavailability of facilities. Also, they race frequently, and weight training would slow their recovery.

I have tried it both ways with mixed results. If I continue to do squats when I'm riding hard, the danger of overtraining is always present. It takes longer for my legs to recover and I can't quite do as much quality work on my bike. On the other hand, my strength remains high and I seem to have more power.

Don't be dismayed if the weight you can handle in the squat drops in the spring when you begin to ride more. This is a common

Continue light upper-body workouts twice a week into the racing season. Abdominal and lower back muscles help transfer energy from hips and thighs to pedals.

phenomenon. Exercise physiologist Dr. David Costill studied a world-class marathoner who had a maximum oxygen uptake value of 78, but whose vertical jump (a good indicator of power) was only nine inches. Tested again after a four-year layoff from running, his oxygen uptake decreased to 47, but his vertical jump increased to 22 inches. How can four years of not training produce such improvement? Apparently, endurance training saps the power measured by the vertical jump or squat.

A year-round program

Here is a general year-round weight training plan for the cyclist. It is based on the theory of periodization that is recommended by U.S. Olympic coach Eddie Borysewicz and many other coaches. Be sure to vary the workouts within each segment; don't do the same squat routine six weeks in a row.

October 1 - November 15: Do a general program for the whole body. Use fairly light weights, one to three sets, and a wide variety of exercises. Don't go to maximum. Keep the physical and mental stress moderate because the purpose is to work all the muscles and prepare them for more intensive work later.

November 15 - January 1: Circuit training. In most climates it is hard to ride much during this period because of darkness, bad weather, or both. Vigorous circuit training takes up some of the aerobic slack caused by time off the bike, and it is more strenuous than the light training you did in October.

January 1 - February 15: Power phase for the legs. Start building up your power with three to five sets of squats using 10-25 repetitions. It's preferable to do the squat workout only twice a week — say, on Tuesday or Thursday, and maybe again on Sunday — on the days when you are also doing hard riding on the wind-load simulator or on the road. This gives your legs plenty of time to recover from the hard days. If you work them hard with squats one day and ride hard the next, recovery time is too short. The idea is to really blitz the legs with squats and power work on the bike all in one day, then let them recover fully before you do it again.

Alternate upper-body workouts with squats, usually doing them on Monday and Friday, if those are the days when you'll be taking it easy after hard-riding days. Increase upper-body strength using the "one set to exhaustion" method to save time and energy needed for the legs to adapt.

February 15 - April 1: Retain the one-set upper-body workouts on Monday and Friday, and squats on Tuesday and Sunday. Change the squat workout to three to five sets of up to 50 reps with lighter weights to increase your power.

April 1 - October 1: Light upper-body workouts twice a week on days when you ride easily on the bike. Leg work in the form of squats is optional depending on whether your experience has shown that it helps you get stronger or makes you tired. In any case, discontinue weight work for the legs at least two weeks before major events where you want to be at your best.

6.
Exercise selection and execution

As a racing cyclist you probably engage in a weight training program, at least during the off-season. But are you realizing maximum benefits in strength development? A successful program must be tailored to your needs as a cyclist in general as well as to your individual requirements. If you lack snap in your legs, it makes little sense to key on bench presses simply because you are training with a body builder. You must also integrate your strength program into your overall training regimen so that your abilities as a cyclist are enhanced, not diminished. Time management is crucial since the actual amount of time spent off the bike is limited when you are training year-round.

This chapter will tell you some of the exercises you should include in your program. A coach or a book on weightlifting may be of help in learning specific techniques.

Although there are hundreds of weight training movements a cyclist can employ in a training program, basic exercises should provide the framework of your routine. Your training should emphasize integrated, multiple-joint movements rather than isolation exercises (although there is clearly a role for these specialized exercises).

Your weight program should be fairly specific to the demands of bicycle racing. To effectively simulate cycling, you may need to adapt old movements and invent some new exercises.

Specificity of training means not only imitating the movements of cycling, but also the speed of those movements. Training at low velocities increases strength primarily at lower velocities while training at high velocities develops both high- and low-velocity strength. This has implications for athletes who train on cam-type machines, which are designed for low-velocity movements.

Exercises that will not specifically aid your performance as a cyclist can be excluded from your program — unless you intend to devote an exceptional amount of time to the weight room. Few cyclists need to spend as much time with weights as power athletes do.

Your main goals are to develop what's called speed-strength and to improve the condition of connective tissue (tendons and ligaments). The desired result is a significant increase in your strength-to-body-weight ratio. Hypertrophy, or increase in muscle size, should be considered an undesirable side effect. Increased muscle mass is probably a disadvantage to most road cyclists and is frequently mentioned as a reason for cyclists to avoid weight training. However, muscular development can be minimized by carefully developing your program.

Your training program should focus on three major body regions: hips and legs; trunk; and pulling muscles of the shoulders, arms, and upper back. Supplementary work is directed at the neck area. Areas of lesser importance are the chest and pushing muscles of the upper body.

Hips and legs

The basic movement for strengthening this area is squatting. Back squats generally form the backbone of any strength program. The back squat is more a hip extension movement than a leg extension movement. As such it works the gluteals, hamstrings, and spinal erectors. The quadriceps are certainly involved, but they can be trained more effectively with the front squat.

Leg pressing on various machines will also strengthen this area. When using leg press machines, be certain to adjust them so that you can either work through a complete range of motion or at least through the range your hips and knees experience while pedaling. Another approach to working this area is to perform step-ups on a box. Resistance is provided by placing a barbell across your shoulder blades or by holding dumbbells in your hands.

To train the hip extension function of the hamstrings (the major role of the hamstrings in cycling) you can include standing hip

Here's how to do squats

Position of barbell in back squat: Step in toward the squat racks. Step under the bar and position it across your shoulder blades. Grip should be comfortable and secure. Note that a wide grip will cause you to lean forward; a narrow grip will help you keep erect.

Position of barbell in front squat: Step in toward the racks. Grasp the bar with an overhead grip slightly wider than shoulder width. (Flexibility is important.) The bar should sit at the junction of your palm and fingers. Rotate your elbows under the bar until they point almost directly forward. The weight should be supported by your shoulders and collarbone, not your wrists and hands. Your wrists should be fairly flexible.

Foot spacing: Your feet should be spaced slightly wider than hip width, with toes angled slightly out and heels under your hips. This position may be modified for comfort, but try not to go to extremes.

Descent: Keep your head slightly up, lock your back, throw out your chest, and inhale. The descent should be done in a controlled manner — better too slow than too fast. A rapid descent increases the risk of knee and lower-back injuries. Try to maintain a fairly erect posture; don't lean too far forward. If you have difficulty staying erect, you may lack sufficient ankle flexibility. Use shoes with heels or place a plate under your heel (not under your instep).

Depth: The tops of your thighs should be below a line drawn parallel to the floor through your knees. It's not necessary to squat much deeper; if your squat is too shallow you don't work the glutes as much. Once you reach the proper depth take care not to stop or bounce — both of these mistakes may lead to injury.

Ascent: Upon reaching the proper depth, begin the ascent. Exhale as you rise. Your ascending velocity should be faster than your descending velocity — considerably faster if you wish to develop speed-strength.

extension exercises in your program. These are done with either an iron boot or a pulley apparatus, and involve pulling the knee up and extending the foot outwards from a standing position. Nautilus has a hip/back machine that trains this movement.

Knee flexion strength is usually developed by doing leg curls. For better overall development of the muscles that make up the hamstrings, vary the angle of toe-in and toe-out from set to set. Leg curls should be done at a fairly high velocity to train the fast-twitch muscle fibers that predominate in this muscle group.

Although the quads are trained by squats and leg presses, leg extension exercises do a better job in isolating this muscle group. They can be done either on a machine or with an iron boot.

Full-range leg extensions may put undue stress on your knee, due to improper tracking of the kneecap. (Don't diagnose it yourself. See a physician.) To avoid the problem, limit extension to the upper range of motion. When done this way, the exercise is known as a lockout. It helps strengthen the medial vastus muscle (one of the quads), whose function is to stabilize the kneecap. Lockouts may also be performed over a smaller range of motion as an isometric exercise (contract for six seconds, relax for four — complete 10 reps). Partial leg extensions over the first third of the range of motion may also be useful.

Hip flexion strength can be developed using iron boots and performing hip flexion exercises. (In a standing position, the leg is lifted upwards with the knee bent.) Hydra-Gym manufactures a hip flexion machine.

Muscles of the calf (particularly the tibialis anterior, which flexes the ankle) come into play during cycling. To strengthen the tibialis, use isometrics, pulley exercises, or inner-tube exercises. The extensor muscles of the calf can be worked with various forms of heel raises. When doing heel raises, place your toes on a board, vary the angle of your feet, and get a full range of motion.

To help develop explosiveness, movements such as power cleans (weight to chest height), power snatches (weight over the head),or high pulls should be included in your program. High pulls are the initial movement of the power clean or snatch — but the elbows never pass under the bar.

In the *Weightlifter's Newsletter,* Denis Reno offers the following simple explanation of how to perform the power clean: "Plant

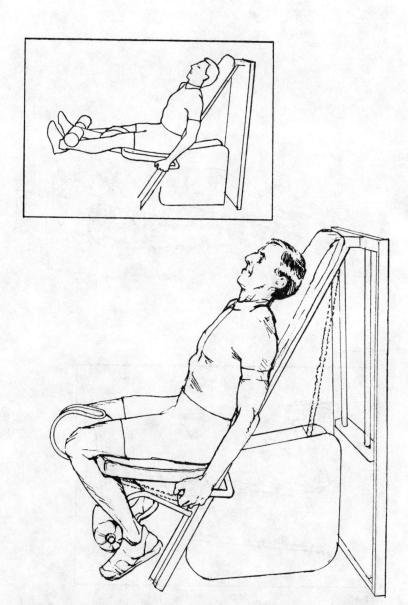

The Nautilus leg extension machine or an iron boot can be used to work the quadriceps. To avoid stress on your knees you may want to limit the range of motion in leg extensions.

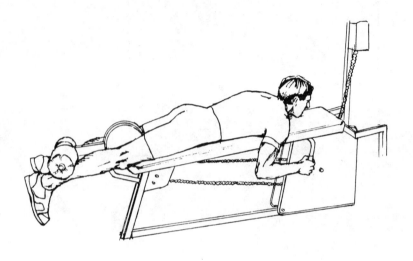

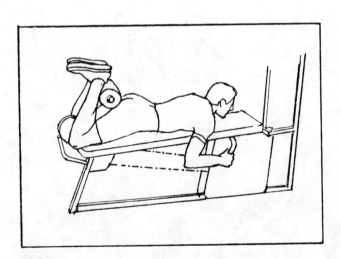

Leg curls, done with an iron boot or on a Nautilus machine, develop knee flexion strength and the hamstrings. Vary the angle of the foot from set to set and do them at a fairly high velocity.

your feet solidly on the platform as though you are going to do a high forward jump. Take a grip slightly wider than shoulder width and make sure that your chest is over the bar. Now push the floor with your feet, turning your elbows as the bar reaches your chest height.''

If you still have problems, remember: 1. Keep your knuckles along your body during the complete pull. 2. Keep your elbows to your side and your arms relaxed. 3. Rotate your elbows as the bar reaches your lower chest level.

The high pull (using straps to secure your hands to the bar) can be more easily learned and will stress the wrists less than cleans or snatches. This may be the better way to go. In any event, you must remember that these pulling movements are essentially vertical jumps with a barbell in your hands. They are not reverse curls.

Trunk

The two main muscle groups of the trunk — the spinal erectors and the abdominals — can be trained with squats, cleans, and snatches. However, there are other specific exercises for this area of the body.

Crunches (or trunk curls), with the knees bent and the legs unsupported, train the upper abdominal muscles. (Remember, the effective range of motion for these muscles is the first 30-40 degrees; beyond that hip flexors come into play.) To increase resistance, hold a barbell across the chest (not behind the head).

The lower abdominals are worked by flexing the lower trunk, pulling your knees into your chin. To increase resistance, do these on an adjustable sit-up board. Side bends with a dumbbell develop lateral flexion strength. Rotational strength can be developed by adding twisting motions to crunches and pull-ins. (Pull-ins involve bringing the knees to the chest while on an incline board.) Even better than these two movements is the Russian twist, in which you lean back slightly while sitting in the hyperextension chair and twist the upper body.

Hyperextensions (back raises), Good Mornings (bend-overs), and the pulling exercises mentioned above all strengthen the spinal erectors of the lower back. Hyperextensions are safer than Good Mornings. Do them without actually hyperextending (stop when you are parallel to the floor). With either exercise, don't do too much too fast — a lower-back injury can really set you back. Treat these exercises with respect.

To develop rotational strength in the lower back, load weight on one end of the barbell only, bend forward and twist (weighted side goes down, then up in a twisting fashion).

Upper body

Since the upper torso primarily pulls on the handlebars, pulling — not pushing (pressing) — exercises should be emphasized. Upright rowing, using either a barbell or dumbbells, works the upper arms, shoulders, and upper back. Bent-over rowing (medium to narrow grip) and lateral bar/pulley rowing will also work your upper back and arms. Movements such as lat pulldowns and wide-grip chins should be avoided since they contribute to the development of a wider upper body — hardly aerodynamic. Pressing movements need not be excluded, but they should form a small portion of your training load.

There seems to be little need to do isolation exercises for the arms. The biceps are involved in all of the pulling movements, including the rowing exercises. And if you include presses, the triceps will be affected.

Neck

Since your neck may bear the brunt of the impact in a crash, it makes sense to spend some time conditioning that area. Fortunately, the neck usually responds very well to training. If you lack the more sophisticated equipment (such as Nautilus machines), other movements such as headstrap exercises, isometrics, and bridging will work quite well. Remember to train the front, back, and sides. With Nautilus, you can even train rotation. This is another body area that should not be pushed too hard in the early stages of a program.

7.
The annual strength training cycle

Many strength programs for novices are quite basic and designed to achieve improvements only during the off-season. Such short-term, high-intensity programs carry the risk of injury and may lead to plateaus in your training. While a long-term approach may be less dramatic, your body will be given the opportunity to adapt to the increased training loads needed to develop strength.

Younger and older cyclists must take particular care to regulate the amount of high-intensity weight training — younger athletes because of the risk to growing bones, and over-40 riders because of their less-resilient tendons and ligaments.

Cycled training

Since the '70s, the concept of cycled, or periodized, training has been in vogue as a long-term training philosophy. A cycle is made up of several training periods, each designed to develop a specific quality. Within each period there are progressive increases in training stress coupled with carefully placed recovery sessions.

The length of a cycle is usually the full season, but within that there are several partial cycles lasting 6-12 weeks. The four general phases or periods of the full cycle are preparation, strength development, competition, and active recovery.

Each phase uses different volumes and intensities. Volume is either the total amount of weight lifted or the total number of repetitions — whether for a specific exercise or an entire workout. Intensity is the average weight that you lift — usually expressed as a percentage of your best single effort. (This can be calculated by doing a submaximal effort. For instance, if you reached your maximum in the back squat with six reps at 200 pounds, your single-rep maximum would be 235 pounds.)

The preparation period can start about two to three weeks after your last major race (or the end of the season) and last four to six weeks. The goals of this period are similar to those of early-season riding: to build a training base. The emphasis is on learning the movements and working through the muscle soreness you are bound to experience.

Increase volume more than intensity during this period. But don't begin with a high-volume program. Work toward it. Intensity does increase, but not as rapidly as volume. Toward the end of the preparation period, volume begins to decline while intensity keeps going up.

Select four or five exercises (in addition to those for the abdominals) and do them three times each week. Complete about 10 reps per set with a weight light enough that you can lift it 20 times. If you are a complete novice, try two sets for the first two workouts and three to four sets for the next two. Then increase the number of sets to five or six, lifting somewhat heavier weights the last two sets. You should complete all the reps easily and in good form.

After these initial workouts, gradually increase the weight (intensity) while maintaining fairly high reps. At the end of the preparation phase, do a light workout and test yourself on key exercises. The results will be used in the next phase.

Strength development

Strength development is the next phase, and it can last five to seven weeks. The object is to increase intensity, so volume declines. Do 2-6 reps at 75-85% of maximum.

The competition phase is about one week long. This is where you evaluate progress by again testing yourself on key exercises. Remember — this is done with submaximal efforts rather than single repetition lifts with your maximum. There is no compelling reason for a cyclist to risk heavy single efforts.

The volumes at this time will be fairly low and the intensities high. (A similar approach is used during the racing season, where the goal is maintenance rather than strength development.)

Many U.S. sprinters, including former world champion Connie Young, left, use weights extensively in their training.

During the active recovery phase, both volume and intensity are low. This period, which lasts about a week, is crucial to minimize overtraining. Then new and heavier training weights are established based upon your testing.

These three last phases can be repeated as a kind of mesocycle — you should be able to complete two or three of them during the off-season. Track riders may elect to continue strength development further into the season than road racers, who will change to a maintenance program (see separate chapter).

The weekly schedule

Three to four weight training sessions per week are fairly standard for an off-season program, and two sessions per week are recommended for maintenance.

During the off-season, structure your program so that you can complete all exercises in less than two hours. One and a half hours would be better in order to leave time for aerobic training and to avoid a feeling of staleness.

Because of time considerations, you should base your workouts around two to three major exercises. These are multiple-joint movements involving large-muscle groups. They will generally require a good warm-up period and may require spotters.

When these exercises are completed, move on to isolation movements. To save time, you can do these exercises as a circuit. Because the average intensities will be higher than those normally used in circuit training (75-85% of maximum vs. 40-60%) you will not be able to rush through a series.

Alternate hard and easy days. Recovery workouts must be scheduled; if you wait until you feel overtrained it may be too late. The conservative approach is to alternate hard and easy days, but you may be able to do two hard days before training down. In addition, some coaches recommend a light week after every two to three heavy weeks. Intelligent scheduling of recovery days will help you maintain progress over the long term.

8.
Technique and other tips

There are a number of things you should keep in mind as your weight program gets under way. One of the first is technique. If your technique is inadequate, strength gains will be limited and your perception of your strength will be distorted. Have you ever seen someone do a bench press by bouncing the bar off the chest, arching the back, and extending the arms unevenly? Is a lift completed in this manner indicative of your real strength? No way.

With improper technique you risk injury and may reinforce any strength imbalances you may have. The importance of lifting safely and efficiently cannot be overemphasized.

If you have the choice of whether to begin training on machines or with free weights, my recommendation is to choose free weights. They will help you develop motor skills not required by machines. In addition, it is difficult to develop what's called speed-strength on some types of machines. (However, isokinetic machines are useful in developing speed).

Since motor skills and the development of balanced strength are invaluable to athletes, it makes little sense to use machines as the basis of your program. If you switch to machines at a later date, your skills and strength may transfer better than if you did it the other way around.

The training log
Just as you keep a log of your training rides and races, so should you log your strength training. This is especially important in

preventing overtraining. It is much easier to overtrain on power/strength programs than it is to overtrain aerobically.

Accurate record keeping will make it easier to head off staleness and injury and will give you the best feedback on how well you are mixing your strength work with your road training.

One approach is to simply list each exercise, the weight, and the number of repetitions in each set. For instance, with the back squat you might have the following entry:

Back squat: 135/5 135/5 185/5 225/3.

In the same way, monitor resting heart rate and body weight.

Every four to eight weeks, test yourself on key exercises. Since single-rep maximum efforts are unimportant to a cyclist, your tests should be done at 2-5 reps with a submaximal weight. Then project the results to a single-rep max.

Only by measuring your progress (but not too often) will you be able to maintain progress over the long haul. Your approach should be systematic, not haphazard.

Before each session, do a general warm-up including light calisthenics, static stretching, and an easy, short jog. A more specific warm-up should precede each major exercise or the first exercise for any muscle group. This consists of two to four sets of light weights (40-60% of maximum). At the conclusion of your workout do some more static stretching.

Number of repetitions

Many people assume that to develop muscular endurance one should train with light weights at high reps. However a 1982 study found that a high intensity/low-rep program (three sets of 6-8 reps) developed almost as much absolute muscular endurance as did regular workouts using higher reps (two sets of 30-40 reps). And the latter program was less effective for strength development.

What does this imply? If you train for strength you should see an improvement in muscular endurance. But if you train for endurance, your strength gains will be reduced.

Another argument exists for using low reps. For athletes, development of power, or speed-strength, is often more important than development of strength. Too many reps may slow down the speed of the exercise, and develop the wrong kind of strength (low-velocity).

Olympic gold medalist Steve Hegg and other national team members have coaches like Eddie Borysewicz to help in their weight programs. If you don't have a coach, at least try to get some expert advice on technique to help avoid injury and get the maximum benefit from your workouts.

During the first three to six weeks of your program, the number of reps should be fairly high (10-20 per set). As your strength develops, decrease the number of reps to 2-6 per set.

How much weight?

During the first three to six weeks, the weights should be light. If you wish to include circuit training in your program, this is the obvious place for it. During the latter stages of this preparation phase, weights should increase but still be fairly light (65-70% of maximum).

Later, as you develop strength, the average intensities range from 75-85% of maximum, with the intensity of individual sets somewhat higher. Juniors and those without much weight training experience should keep their intensities somewhat lower and the reps higher.

When you actually begin keying on strength development, the average intensities must show a general increase. Without increasing the stimulus to the body you will not gain in strength.

Vary the intensity/rep combinations for each specific exercise within each workout. Consider two workouts, each with the same volume and average intensity:

1. 75% x 5 reps x 5 sets
2. 70% x 6 x 2; 75% x 1 x 5; 80% x 4 x 2

Workout No. 2 offers your body more variety than workout No. 1, and it requires more adaptation, which results in strength improvement.

If you are an inexperienced lifter or if you are in the first three to six weeks of a program, you should control the velocity of your exercises to minimize the risk of injury. Only after you have developed a training base and strengthened your tendons and ligaments should you consider using explosive movements.

Because low-velocity movements do not develop high-velocity strength, it is important to develop a training base so that you can begin to include faster movements in your routine. If you are a novice, use the first year of your program to develop a strength base. In the second year begin to include some faster movements such as power cleans.

Circuit training

Because circuit training uses such low-intensity weights (40-60% of maximum), it gives only modest gains in strength. Furthermore, the value of circuit training in improving oxygen uptake is minimal, even among the untrained. One study found that there was no change in either resting or recovery heart rates after 20 weeks of circuit training.

But circuit training can be useful during the first few weeks of a program. For maximum benefit, keep the rest period between stations brief. (In a busy gym this might prove difficult.)

The bottom line? If your goals are to increase strength (and that is what weight training does best) circuit training is not the best approach.

9.
Speed-strength

Most riders know you won't get fast by riding long distances at a constant speed. The same logic applies to your strength training program. Once you have developed some strength through basic weight training, you can to tailor your program to the special needs of racing.

So called speed-strength is one quality you can emphasize in your workouts. It aids in your escape from the pack — or enables you to chase down someone else's attack.

Speed-strength training differs considerably from other strength training methods. The weights used are generally light — 20-30% of your maximum — and the gains in muscle mass are limited. The number of repetitions are comparatively high (between five and 20), as are the number of sets (four to six).

Speed-strength training demands fast movements. Jumping motions in particular are recommended, since they transfer very nicely to the hip and knee extension movements of cycling.

In designing your program, it's best to integrate speed-strength training into your regular strength training program, rather than train for speed alone. If you abandon basic strength development during speed-strength training, your absolute strength will decline, and vice-versa.

Jumping back squat
The basic speed-strength movement is the jumping back squat. These can be inserted into your program after a very thorough warm-up or after you have completed your heavier squats. (You should have mastered the technique of the regular back squat before trying this exercise.)

Escaping from the pack — like Moreno Argentin did in winning the 1986 professional road championship — takes speed-strength, developed with light weights and fast movements.

A   B   C   D   E   F   G

Cushion your neck by rolling a towel around the center of the barbell or slipping a length of plastic pipe insulation over the bar. Hold the bar on your shoulder blades so it won't crash down on the back of your neck during the jump. Use an absorbent surface (mats) and always have two spotters.

As with the regular squat, you should descend under control with a locked lower back. When you reach the bottom position (thighs parallel to the ground) spring up without bouncing at the bottom. Continue the ascent until you have completed a vertical jump.

Power snatch

A second exercise for explosiveness is the power snatch. The key to this lift (and the closely related power clean) is to treat it as vertical jump done with a barbell in your hand.

First, grasp the bar with palms facing you. The distance between your index fingers should be about the same as that between your elbows when your arms are outstretched. Set your feet hip-width apart (or closer) with toes angled slightly outwards. Stand erect with the bar.

Figure A: Lock your lower back and set your balance toward the balls of your toes. Bend at the hips and knees as shown until the bar is about knee height. Elbows should be rotated outwards, arms relaxed. You should be in a strong position for a vertical jump.

Figures B-D: As soon as the bar drops to knee height, begin the upward pull by driving the hips forward and up as shown. Keep the bar close to your body. Use your legs and hips as you would while jumping.

Figure E: As the height of the bar increases, you may have to bend the arms slightly. To do this, bend the elbows out, not back. Jump about 15-30cm across the floor.

Figures F-G: Continue pulling the bar until it is locked overhead. Catch the bar as you descend into a half squat.

Practice this sequence slowly at first then graduate to a snappy and smooth movement.

Plyometrics

A third kind of speed-strength exercise is a plyometric drill such as depth jumping. Merely step off a box and, upon landing, immediately jump as high as you can.

The height of the box varies with the objective of the drill. For speed, 70cm is ideal; for strength, 110cm. Since this is a very stressful exercise, do it only after you have an extensive strength training base. Do two to four sets of 10 reps, once or twice a week.

Because your knees absorb such large forces on impact, you should wear absorbent shoes and jump onto several layers of mats. Also, these exercises are usually done without additional weight.

There are other plyometric drills besides depth jumps, and you can consult a knowledgeable coach or one of the books now available on the subject for more information.

10.
Trunk strength

Although the muscles of the trunk are not directly involved in pedaling, they help transfer energy from the hips and thighs to the pedals and are used to help fix your position on the bike.

There are three major muscle groups in the trunk that affect cycling: the abdominals, obliques, and lower-back muscles. You can condition these muscles with simple exercises and a minimum of equipment — a weight bar, an incline board, and perhaps a hyperextension chair.

Abdominals

The abdominals are the prime movers when you bend your upper body. The upper abdominals can be trained by curling or crunching your upper torso while lying on the floor with your knees bent or with your feet hanging over a bench. With your feet up on a bench, the abdominals are worked throughout the full range of movement. In either case, your feet should not be held down.

If you do crunches with your feet on the floor, it isn't necessary to do a full sit-up. We know that the abdominals are activated only during the first 45 degrees of flexion. Therefore, the crunch should proceed only until your trunk is flexed 30-45 degrees.

Note that trunk flexion is distinct from hip flexion. Hip exercises include conventional sit-ups and leg raises. These exercises can cause hyperextension of the lumbar spine and may result in lower-back pain. Once your legs begin to leave the floor you have curled your trunk far enough — you are now beginning to involve the thigh muscles. Even with your knees flexed you activate the hip muscles, but they are at a mechanical disadvantage because they are shortened.

Trunk strength is important to developing the power needed for time trialing. This is the 1986 world championship four-man team from Holland.

An isometric contraction at the conclusion of the crunch (for three to five seconds) gives additional benefit. But again, if your ankles are supported, there is greater involvement of the hip flexors and increased curvature of the lumbar spine. You can make crunches more difficult by holding a barbell across the chest.

The lower abdominals can be worked by lifting the hips off the floor when flexing the trunk. Pull your knees to your face, keeping them close to your body. Contract your abdominal muscles when the movement is completed.

To increase the difficulty, use an adjustable slant board and vary the angle of inclination. This exercise may also be done hanging from a chinning bar.

The trunk

Trunk extension depends upon the contraction of the spinal erector muscles — the group of muscles that run parallel to your vertebral column.

If you have a solid training base of hyperextensions you can try the Good Morning, which exercises the lower back and stretches the hamstrings.

Among the simplest and safest lower-back exercises is the hyperextension. Lie face down on a bench (or chair apparatus) with your trunk hanging off the bench from the hips forward. A training partner should hold you down by lying across your ankles. Alternatively, a seatbelt or weightlifting belt may be used to hold you down.

Clasp your hands behind your head and lower your trunk by bending forward at the hips until you are perpendicular to the floor. Raise your upper body, stopping when your trunk is parallel to the floor.

Note that the name of the exercise is misleading; if you actually hyperextend, you can stress your lumbar vertebrae.

Perform the downward part of the exercise in a controlled manner. Do the upward part of the exercise slowly until you have conditioned yourself to the movement. To increase resistance, hold barbell plates or a loaded barbell across your back at the top of your shoulder blades. (Do not support the weights across the back of your neck.) To develop some rotational strength, twist to one side on alternate contractions.

The Good Morning exercise is also good for the lower back, and it can also be useful in stretching the hamstrings. Position a light barbell across your shoulder blades and stand erect with your feet about hip width apart. Slowly bend forward at the hips. Keep your knees either straight or slightly flexed, your back arched and locked or rounded. Generally, you will find it easier (and probably safer) if your knees are slightly bent and your back is locked (chest thrown out, back slightly hyperextended, and spinal erectors contracted). Once your trunk is parallel to the floor, return to the erect position.

Approach this exercise with respect. If you bend over too quickly, if the weight is too heavy, or if the bar is positioned across your neck, there is a good chance that you will injure yourself. In fact, I don't recommend this exercise unless the trainee has a solid training base of hyperextensions.

To develop rotational strength, modify the Good Morning by loading plates on only one side of the barbell and performing a twisting movement while bent forward.

Oblique muscles
The oblique muscles (lateral flexion and rotation) may be trained

with side bends. Hold a dumbbell in one hand, flex to the side of the weight, then flex to the opposite side. Then switch the weight to the other hand to train your opposite side.

Rotational strength may be developed by adding twisting movements to your crunches. The Russian twist, a backward leaning motion done in the hyperextension chair, is also effective.

How much and when?

How should you work these movements into your strength training program? In the off-season, try to perform four to six sets (after completing one to three lighter warm-up sets) with your training weights. Initially emphasize increases in training volume (total weight lifted or total repetitions) over increases in intensity (average weight).

Develop your base over three to six weeks using light weights at high (10-20) reps. After this preparation period, go to a strength development period in which you train at higher intensities (75-85% of your estimated one-rep maximum).

Vary your intensities so that there is an increase in training intensity over a six- to ten-week cycle. In addition, include light training days so that every other (or every third) trunk workout is at a low intensity and volume.

For example, your heavy days may show a progression in average intensity from 75-85% over an eight-week period; your light days might fall every third session and the intensity might be 60-65%.

In the off-season, do one session per week devoted to the trunk. Freehand abdominal exercises should be done more often.

11.
In-season
maintenance

Although many cyclists spend considerable time during the off-season building up muscular strength for the racing season, only track riders seem to regularly include weight training as part of their in-season regimen. Think about it — you invest time and energy building up your strength, yet by August and September, when you need it most, your strength will have returned to pre-training levels. That is, unless you devote some time to maintain that strength.

Of course, if you race several times each week, all your off-bike efforts will be geared towards recuperation. However, developing racers, tourists, and those who compete only on weekends would benefit by continuing their strength training throughout the season.

Weight training needn't take too much time from your cycling. Strength can be maintained with two workouts per week, and these workouts can probably be completed in little more than one hour.

The keys to an effective in-season program are exercise selection and training intensity. You should emphasize exercises such as squats or power cleans, which involve large muscle groups. Some isolation exercises can be used for the legs, abdomen, neck, and back.

Also, your program should emphasize free weights rather than machines (although machine training is useful for certain isolation exercises and injury rehabilitation).

Which workouts will help?
Your program should revolve around those muscle groups

directly involved with riding the bike. For instance, trunk strength is of paramount importance. Your lower-back, abdominal, and hip muscles are used in fixing your position on the bike and are crucial to generating power. Power cleans and clean high pulls work this region quite well.

Squats work the hips and thighs while employing the lower-back and abdominal muscles as stabilizers. If you spend a lot of time riding out of the saddle, you should emphasize back squats because they work your glutes — important muscles for that kind of riding.

If you compete mainly on the flats, you may wish to do front squats, which exercise the quadriceps more than the glutes. Here, the barbell is supported on the front part of your shoulders and chest. (Good wrist flexibility is required for this lift.)

Cyclists often pull on their handlebars when climbing or sprinting. Upright rowing works the arm flexors, shoulders, and upper-back muscles needed for that effort.

Pressing, long a staple in most weight training programs, is a movement not found in cycling and can be excluded.

Isolation exercises

Isolation exercises are useful for the abdomen, back, neck, and legs. Remember that your abdominal muscles are trunk flexors, not hip flexors, so in order to effectively train this area you should concentrate on curling your trunk. Such exercises include crunches, trunk curls, and pulling your knees into your chest and flexing your trunk. Avoid straight-legged sit-ups and leg raises, both of which exercise the hips and not the abdominals.

Hyperextensions, or back raises, will isolate the lower back muscles and are excellent if you take care not to actually hyperextend your back. Raise your back only until it is parallel to the floor.

Leg extensions and hamstring curls may also be included in your program.

Most cyclists tend to neglect the neck, though it often bears the brunt of the punishment in a collision. Isometric or isotonic exercises can strengthen this area. Remember to work the front, back, and sides.

Track riders know the benefits of weight training as part of their in-season regimen. The well-developed East Germans took the top four places in the 1986 world sprint championships. That's fourth place Bill Huck on the left and eventual gold medalist Michael Huebner on the right. Huebner's 26½-inch thighs are a result of weight work.

How fast?

It is important that you do your lifts at the right speed. Power cleans and pulls are explosive movements. If performed properly, they are useful in developing power and quickness. Squatting movements should also be explosive from the bottom up.

Squatting has a bad reputation because many people descend like rockets and get injured. The descent should be controlled and considerably slower than the ascent. By descending under control, you avoid bouncing and relaxation of the lower back, both major causes of squatting injuries.

Hamstring curls and leg extensions should also be performed quickly, since the dominant muscle fibers in these areas respond to rapid, high-intensity movements. This is important since some machine manufacturers specify that only slow movements be done with their machines, without taking into consideration the types of muscle fibers affected by the exercise.

Intensity and volume

The intensity at which you train is a key to maintaining strength. Strength training is high-intensity work, involving weights of 80-85% of your single-repetition maximum. (Weights of 90% and greater are not recommended for the in-season program.)

Weight training volume is another consideration. This is either the total number of repetitions or the total poundage lifted in your workout. Whichever way you measure it, it should not be very high. You should perform 2-6 repetitions per set with weights in the 80-85% zone. Forget about higher reps — you are interested in functional strength and power, not muscularity.

Each exercise should start with several warm-up sets with light weights, then progress to one to three sets at 80-85% of maximum. Here is an example:

One set of 3-4 reps at 50%; one set of 3-4 reps at 60%; one set of 3 reps at 70%; one to three sets of 3 reps at 80%.

If you require more of a warm-up, add a set or two at lower intensities. If you wish to train heavier, go to 85%.

Here is a sample week following the above progression.

Monday:
1. Warm-up: freehand movements, exercises with a very light (or empty) barbell, or static stretches.
2. Power cleans or pulls.
3. Back squats.
4. Abdominal exercises (three to five sets, 10-20 reps per set).
5. Cool-down: static stretching.

Thursday:
1. Warm-up.
2. Upright rowing.
3. Front squats.
4. Abdominal exercises.
5. Cool-down.

Each of these workouts should take less than one hour to complete. Since you are also riding, they should not be overly taxing. If you have the time or inclination, add some isolation movements — but don't get carried away. The object is not

Whether you climb in the saddle or out, upright rowing during the season keeps the pulling muscles in shape. Left to right, some famous climbers: Greg LeMond, who won the '86 Tour de France; Andy Hampsten, fourth that year; and five-time winner Bernard Hinault. (For a closer view of LeMond, see page 34.)

necessarily to get stronger but to retain the strength you already have. If you are peaking for a major race, you should eliminate the last one or two weight sessions prior to your race to be sure you are rested.

Participating in an in-season maintenance program has an additional advantage: Your off-season program can begin with much less soreness and at a higher level than if you had taken the season off.

Recommended reading: *Soviet Sports Review,* published by Dr. Michael Yessis, contains several articles per issue devoted to strength/speed-strength training. The principles can be adapted and applied to the strength training needs of cyclists.

12.
A 22-minute workout

The combination of a working wife, my own career, a small child, and shorter daylight hours in winter has given me an abiding interest in off-season strength development and training. After a competitive athletic career in college and several winters of training with avid weightlifters and body builders, I think I have found a weight program that satisfies most of the criteria for a quality training program enumerated by Stephen Grabe in his articles. It originated in the rowing clubs of the Schuylkill River in Philadelphia and is known as the 22-minute drill.

Exclusive of warm-up and warm-down, the six sets of 10 repetitions of eight exercises are to be done in 22 minutes. The barbell is never put down and the weight on the bar is not changed during the routine.

Because the weights involved are not high, the risk of serious injury is minimized and a spotter is not absolutely necessary. Another advantage of the routine is that you don't need any equipment other than a bar, some weight plates, and a bench or a reasonable substitute.

Depending on your objectives, the goal for the end of the weight training season (mid- to late March) is to get through the routine in as close to 22 minutes as possible using weights that total 40-60% of your body weight. For example, my winter weight is 170 pounds and I am a slightly above average rider (that is, I have never failed to pay my entry fees and travel expenses from prime and prize money at any race). This past October I broke my collarbone so I started the weight lifting season with a bar and plates totaling 40

For the bench press, grip the bar slightly wider than shoulders, lower bar to chest and push back up until arms are straight. Don't bounce the bar off the chest.

pounds. I anticipate hitting last winter's achieved goal of 80 pounds for the routine done in 26 minutes. This may not seem like a lot of weight, but wait until you see what is coming.

A. B.

1.   *Deadlift:* Hands on the bar a little wider than your shoulders and outside your knees. As you do the exercise, keep your eyes on the top edge of the wall about 20 feet opposite. This will keep your back straight and your butt down, essentials for avoiding back injury.

2.   *Bench press:* Do not increase the weight, do not put the bar down. Go straight to the bench, concentrate on form and speed.

3.   *Power clean:* This is described in Grabe's articles and pictured above. The bar goes from the floor to your shoulders in one smooth, clean motion. Again, it is very important to keep your head up and your butt down. If your butt starts to rise faster than your head, you are inviting disaster. Such a movement puts enormous strain in all the wrong places in your back.

4. *Military press:* Everyone knows this one. The bar goes from shoulder height, behind your head, to directly overhead. Keep your back straight so that your shoulders and arms are doing the work.

5. *Squat:* The bar is already at shoulder height and behind your head, so leave it there while you do your squats. Keep your head up and your butt down.

6. *Curls:* Bring the bar over your head and reverse your hands for a set of arm curls. Don't rock and sway to help heave the bar from your waist to your chin.

7. *Burpee clean:* This is the hardest exercise in the group. After your curls, you are vertical with the bar in your hands. Squat down to lower the bar to the floor. Still holding on to the bar, thrust your legs out behind you. The bar is on the floor, you are holding onto it, and you are in a horizontal position facing the floor, arms outstretched. Bring your feet back under you and rise as in a deadlift. In the deadlift of this exercise, all done in a smooth sequence, keep your butt down.

Rows can be vertical or bent-over, as shown here. In this version let the barbell hang just above the floor, pull weight up to chest and lower slowly.

If you are a masochist and your house has sufficient ceiling height you can substitute burpee snatches for the burpee clean. In the snatch, the bar goes from the floor directly overhead in a single clean motion.

ODD SETS   EVEN SETS

8. *Rows:* On the odd-numbered sets do vertical rows, drawing the bar from waist height to chin height and back, with your hands near the center of the bar. On the even-numbered sets do bent-over rows. Bend 90 degrees at the waist with arms hanging straight. Without straightening up, raise the bar to your shoulders. On the bent-over rows pay attention to what your back is saying to you. I have known people to hurt themselves.

What will you get out of exercises with weights that a powerlifter would laugh at? After six sets of 10 repetitions of the eight exercises described above, you will have done 240 repetitions using the major muscle groups of your legs and lower back and 240 repetitions using various muscle groups in your upper body.

To accommodate your objectives you can alter the recommended weight and elapsed time for the routine. Use lower weight and shorter elapsed time for an aerobic workout, or greater weight and longer elapsed time to develop greater strength. The sequence of the exercises is arranged so that you need not ever put the bar down, so you will always get something of an aerobic workout.

Do not ever hold your breath or close your eyes when working out with weights. If you find yourself doing either of these, lower the weight on the bar.

And finally, don't forget your warm-up and warm-down routines. A good warm-up consists of some stretching and calisthenics then five minutes on the rollers. I usually close the session with 25-30 minutes on the rollers, without load-simulation fans, in order to spin and loosen up.

13.
Using Nautilus in your program

Many coaches, including Stephen Grabe, recommend a weight training program using mostly free weights. But what should you do when the local gym features only Nautilus-type machines? Can a Nautilus program benefit the competitive cyclist? What's the best way to use these machines? To find out I asked several weight training experts and coaches.

At a weight center

"It is difficult to simulate on a machine the variety of muscles found in cycling," says Bob Farentinos, who runs an exercise center in Boulder, CO. "The machine is limited. All it can do is increase strength. That's a long way from riding a bicycle."

Farentinos has worked extensively with Andy Hampsten, who in 1985 won the Tour of Switzerland and was fourth in the Tour de France. Hampsten's program includes only two Nautilus machines — the leg curl and the leg extension. "Nautilus works really well for that," says Hampsten. But in general, "it zeros in on one muscle too much, which is not the way cycling is."

"We use Nautilus machines the way we use everything else," says Farentinos. "It's not the master recipe. We apply it according to the program. For weak muscles or rehabilitation we put people on an isolating machine [such as Nautilus], where there is resistance in one plane of movement.

"Machines are convenient — you don't have to use your brain. There is a lack of neuromuscular involvement. They are used primarily by body builders. They were invented years ago by body

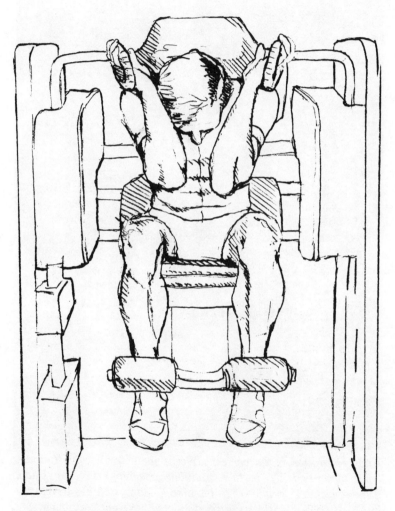

Opinions vary on the value of machines like Nautilus in a weight program. A benefit is their convenience and safety. This is the abdominal machine. Professional triathlete and coach Hank Lange, quoted in this chapter, is the model for the exercise drawings in this book and is seen on the cover.

Andy Hampsten is the perfect advertisement for weight training. Once described by former national coaching director Eddie Borysewicz as "skinnier than his bike," Hampsten has developed into one of the world's top road riders. "Weight training was a real backbone of my training," he said after his successful first season as a pro (1985). "It made me really strong. When the racing season came around I was really fit without being over-trained." In 1986 he won the 11-day Tour of Switzerland and placed fourth in the Tour de France.

builders to fine tune a muscle in terms of shape or size, not to apply that shape or size to athletics. It was strictly for aesthetics.

"If it's all you have, do Nautilus. You can get something out of it." Farentinos recommends two to three sets of 12 repetitions, rather than the single set of 8-12 repetitions that is the standard Nautilus prescription.

"[The Nautilus program] is made for the masses. They say the same thing to everyone. I think you need to work the muscle group much more intensely. I would recommend three sets per muscle, not on the circuit. If you are doing curls, for instance, do three sets at each machine.

"It's too simplistic to say, yes, do 12 to [momentary muscular] failure. That might be good for anaerobic muscle involvement, but in cycling you need mostly aerobic power. And to go fast, you need the explosive power not found in slow reps." (Most Nautilus programs recommend slow rather than fast movements.)

The ski team and triathlete view

Professional triathlete and former national crosscountry ski coach Hank Lange is even more emphatic about doing multiple sets "One set is total BS. I don't know any coaches involved in weight training that have their athletes do one set other than for maintenance."

He recommends three sets, but warns that some Nautilus gyms may not want athletes to spend that much time at the machines. "You can create waves by doing three sets. They want to get you in and out as fast as possible, so you have to go in when you won't mess anyone up. Our crosscountry team goes in at 6:30 a.m."

Lange also warns against the claim that Nautilus-type machines provide a significant aerobic workout. "You can get your heart rate up from a high-force workout, but it's not that aerobic. When they talk about the aerobic benefits of Nautilus they are talking about the recreational athlete who doesn't do anything else."

Lange has developed a Nautilus program for the Keene (NH) State College ski team that emphasizes two types of workouts — either high force or high endurance.

"On Monday and Friday we do one set of 15-25 reps warm-up, stopping short of failure. After 20-30 seconds rest we raise the weight and do a second set still at high reps — about 12-20. Now we are reaching momentary muscle failure at between 12 and 20 reps. The final set is still higher force [more weight] for 4-8 reps. This way you are getting in 40-50 reps on each machine.'' (Lange defines momentary muscle failure as that point at which accessory muscles are brought into play.)

"On Wednesday we do a true high-force set. After the same warm-up set as on Mondays and Fridays, we do one good high-force set using 10-20 pounds more than the final set used on the other days. On Monday you might fail at four or five, whereas on Wednesday you might be able to go to eight or nine with the same weight. It's up to you how you do it.

"With the high-force sets, you end up losing form on one or two reps. I still do those one or two reps partially, so you really reach exhaustion. That is the only place you are allowed to lose form. Everywhere else you are very conscious of form.

"Initially, stay away from three sets in the upper body where you are using smaller muscle groups. Do two sets. And every six weeks you should change the program. With the same program you tend to plateau."

At the OTC

Ed Burke, former director of sportsmedicine, science, and technology for the U.S. Cycling Federation in Colorado Springs, says Nautilus presents "a kind of Catch-22 situation"—while it may not be ideal for the competitive cyclist, there often isn't anything else available. "Here at the Olympic Training Center we have free weights and Universal machines. The disadvantage [of such machines] is that you are locked into one plane of motion, and lots of sports don't function in one plane. You're not going to get the variety you get with free weights. If you can combine it with free weights, that's better."